The Feng Shui Guide to
CLEARING
YOUR SPACE

The Feng Shui Guide to
CLEARING YOUR SPACE

How to unclutter and balance your
environment using feng shui and
other ancient cleansing rituals

ANTONIA BEATTIE

FENG SHUI CONSULTANT – ROSEMARY STEVENS

LANSDOWNE

CONTENTS

Feng Shui and the Art of Space Clearing

In the Chinese belief system, universal energy, or 'qi', is an energy force originating in nature. It is generated by the movement of opposing forces such as heaven and earth, dark and light, male and female. An invisible force, qi circles around and within us. It is thought to have the strength of the wind ('feng') and the undulating ebb and flow of a river ('shui'). Feng shui (pronounced 'foong swee' in Cantonese and 'fong shwee' in Mandarin) is the Chinese art of placement, a holistic system that has been developed over many thousands of years. It is believed to affect every aspect of our lives.

When the qi flowing within us meets a blockage or constriction, disease can take hold. Similarly, if the energy within our living spaces is obstructed by clutter and dirt, we may experience feelings of unease or unbalance — in our lives as well as in particular living areas. In extreme cases, we may sometimes feel so uncomfortable in our own homes that our health is affected.

Feng shui and nature magic

Our lives today are often removed from nature and the wisdom of the natural world, making us feel aimless and unconnected. By tapping into the earth's powerful energy through feng shui, and through some simple nature magic practices, we can link into something bigger than us that can evoke a powerful sense of balance and harmony.

Feng shui uses a sophisticated approach to identify and remedy the stagnant energy within a house. According to its principles, each section of the house (except the center) corresponds to a particular aspect of a person's life, a compass direction and one of the five elements in the Chinese belief system — earth, air, fire, water or wood. Once feng shui practitioners have located the blockage or stagnation in the home, they can readily identify what blockages its residents are experiencing in their love lives, finances, careers and health.

This book gives you fundamental information to help you understand and manage the flow of energy around you in your home and life. By using the principles of feng shui, and by applying the practices of ancient nature magic and the traditions of other cultures to these feng shui principles, you can tap into the wisdom of both East and West. You will gain insight into your life by seeing how the energy flows around you and learn some simple ways to clear the clutter, disharmony and dissatisfaction from your living and working spaces.

WHAT IS SPACE CLEARING?

'Space clearing' refers to the various techniques used to clear negative energy from your home or workplace. It is an amalgam of feng shui techniques and customs from other cultures, such as Tibet, India and Native American tribes. It may also include aspects of nature magic. The main elements of feng shui space clearing involve removing negative energy, increasing beneficial energy, and putting special things in place to enhance the flow of good energy. Clearing techniques, such as the traditional Native American ritual of smudging, have been used for centuries. Many, like spring cleaning, are common practices today. All feng shui principles are about making your home or work space pleasant and healthy. The simple act of cleaning and removing clutter from an area is an important feng shui practice, as it will immediately rid stagnant energy from a space. Apply the techniques outlined in this book to bring the beneficial flow of energy to your space, and not only will your physical space be 'clear', but you will also feel refreshed and vital.

CLEARING SPACES:
WHAT YOU NEED TO KNOW

WHAT SPACE TO CLEAR

In feng shui, clutter is one of the first warning signals of an energy-flow problem in your home. Clutter and dirt block the qi that should flow freely and in graceful curves around your house and garden. Qi can bring good luck, financial rewards and harmonious relationships if it is allowed to flow unimpeded. If the energy stagnates, bad luck and disharmony result. Any place in your home that is cluttered and dusty must be cleared.

Feng shui is concerned not only with obvious clutter, but also with the hidden untidiness that can be found in cupboards, shelves, drawers and under beds. Practitioners believe that clutter that is hidden away, particularly under beds or in the basement, indicates disguised ill health or misfortune. It is important to clear the negative energy.

According to feng shui beliefs, other spaces needing attention are areas hit by 'poison arrows' (see page 13). You will need to learn how to block and cleanse this poisonous energy.

In other belief systems such as nature magic, feelings of discomfort or unease in your home may also correspond to a poor flow of the earth's energy in the house. The cause may be a previous trauma or strong unhappiness. It could also be a disruption in the natural energy of the earth beneath your house. If you sense blockages, you are being neither over-sensitive nor over-imaginative. Go with your feelings, and clear any space in which you feel such negative emotions.

What is Nature Magic?

~

Nature magic is a broad term used to describe some of the magical practices and beliefs of nature-revering people. These include Native Americans and other traditional cultures, as well as Wiccans and some other new age groups. Just as feng shui is concerned with the beneficial flow of energy, nature magic revolves around the energy of the seasons, the phases of the moon and the movement of the planets. It focuses on how we can attune ourselves to the power and balance of this energy and use it to fulfill wishes and live in harmony.

WHEN TO CLEAR YOUR SPACE

Feng shui practitioners use a yearly Chinese calendar that lists lucky and unlucky days. It also lists the best days for house cleaning. However, clutter can also be cleared gradually; it is not vital to clear negative energy in one go. Prioritize the areas you would like to clear; check pages 12–13 to see how a problem in your life could be solved by focusing on the clutter in one particular area.

In nature magic, magical work is done using the energy of the seasons and the phases of the moon. Spring, traditionally the time of a new cycle of growth and the symbol of renewal, is the best time for clearing negative energy from your home. Smaller clearing projects — for example, the feng shui principle of clearing the clutter from under your bed — should be carried out, according to nature magic, during the phase of the new moon. This, like spring, is symbolic of fresh beginnings.

USING SPACE CLEARING TECHNIQUES

The benefits of space clearing are manifold. They include:
- reducing stress and discomfort
- improving sleep patterns
- achieving greater balance and harmony
- clearing of old emotional hurts that act as obstacles in your life
- opening the way for fresh new opportunities, and for abundance.

Space clearing is a growing art. Many space clearing techniques used by cultures such as Tibet, India and Native American tribes, and by nature magic practitioners, share a common thread with feng shui, in that all such practices developed through the observation of nature over many centuries.

Tapping into the universal energy force is common to many traditional practices. Nature magic practices tap into the earth's energy by living in harmony with nature. Clearing techniques, such as smudging, drumming, clapping and purification with salt water, are taken from both feng shui and from the practices of other cultures.

When seeking to integrate Eastern and Western philosophies, find out where possible why a certain belief evolved, and make your own decision as to whether to adopt it. Use your intuition when choosing the best course to take in your house, and follow what feels right to you. This book offers suggestions from feng shui, nature magic practices and the wisdom of other ancient cultures.

A number of the observations in feng shui have correlations with the wisdom of other cultures. For example, many cultures believe that using melodious sounds can aid the flow of energy in a stagnant area of your home. In feng shui, five-rod metal chimes are particularly useful in stimulating qi, particularly in the area of your house or workplace that responds to mentors and travel. Chimes can also be used to attract abundance. Choose whatever melodious sounds you wish. You may be attracted to crystal singing bowls, Tibetan cymbals called tingshas or even Mayan bells.

With space clearing, the aim is to develop your sensitivity to the energy or 'atmosphere' around you. The techniques you use can be chosen according to your own intuition, circumstances and belief system. You can use any technique that appeals to you to give you insight into the negativity that is felt in your home.

When using feng shui only, practitioners often recommend that you don't make too many corrections to the energy at once. If you decide to try both feng shui and nature magic concepts, it is suggested that you use only one practice at a time, and wait for a full cycle of the moon before trying another. Use your judgment, and enjoy the feeling of improved connection with the energy of your home and garden.

The sections that follow detail possible techniques using feng shui principles, Native American rituals, and nature magic.

Ten fundamental principles of feng shui have a bearing on space clearing:

Principle 1: A universal energy called 'qi' flows between heaven and earth, around and within human beings and all other living things, as well as around inanimate human-made objects.

Principle 2: The flow of 'qi' within human beings connects us to the energy of the earth and the cosmos. This connection links the quality of our lives to the universal energy in all its manifestations: a gentle flow, stagnation or a rush.

Principle 3: Certain areas of the home and garden correspond with certain aspects of a human being's life, called the 'Aspirations of Life'. These are:
• wealth
• fame and acknowledgment
• relationships
• family and health
• creativity and children
• knowledge and study
• career
• helpful friends, mentors and travel.

Principle 4: Each aspiration corresponds with, among other things, a compass direction, a color, a number, and one of the Chinese elements – earth, air, fire, water and metal. (Earth, as the center of the house, is not connected with an aspiration.)

Principle 5: A number of systems have evolved to show the correlation between these aspirations and a person's house. The simplest system is the grid reproduced below, derived from the 'Bagua':

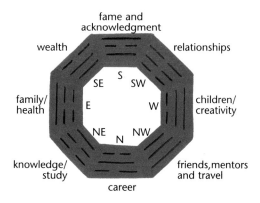

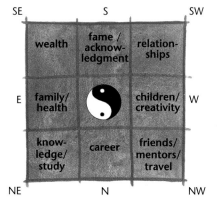

The bagua represents the eight directions (the eight trigrams of the I Ching). Each corresponds to eight life situations (see Principle 3). The bagua is represented in an octagonal shape showing the eight trigrams, with unbroken lines representing yang and broken lines representing yin. It can be drawn as a square with eight sections and sometimes the tai chi (yin yang) symbol is placed in the middle.

Principle 6: Qi flowing in gentle curves brings benefits, such as good luck, harmony, abundance and happy relationships, and keeps the space around us clear. A room where qi flows beneficially gives a feeling of lightness and is a pleasure to use. Its feeling of harmony will match an aspiration in your life.

Principle 7: When qi is blocked, there is stagnation. A room with stagnation (possibly caused by clutter) will give a feeling of discomfort and will seldom be used. The feeling of disharmony will correlate with an aspiration. This stagnation can be remedied by using one of the eight 'cures' (see Principle 10).

Principle 8: If the qi is made to flow too quickly, a strong, forceful energy called a 'poison arrow' is created. It produces a feeling of disharmony where it hits the house or room. Poison arrows can be created by sharp angles from neighboring buildings, telegraph poles, straight lines such as roads and driveways leading to your front door, or long corridors in the house. They can be remedied by using one of the cures listed at Principle 10.

Principle 9: The flow of qi is affected by the shape of a house, the shape of the block of land it sits upon and the environment around it, such as the position of trees, water features, mountains, and electromagnetic fields. Qi flows into your house through the front door. It flows around heavy furniture and slows down through plants, metal chimes and bamboo flutes.

Principle 10: One of the most important ways of correcting poor energy flows is by using 'cures' or lucky objects. There are different types of cures: color; lights; mirrors and crystals; metal chimes and bells; plants and pets; mobiles and flags; statues and rocks; fans and flutes; music.

A Native American Clearing Ritual

Smudging is a Native American traditional clearing ritual. Smudging refers to the burning of certain herbs to cleanse or 'clear' people, objects, rooms and spaces of negative energy and influences. Contemporary practice is heavily influenced by Native American usage, with its earth-centered philosophy and reverence for all living things. American Indians from throughout the Americas, from the Maya and Aztecs, to the Plains Indians, to the aboriginal peoples of Canada, have all employed the smoke of various herbs for help in entering the sacred realm, or to carry prayers to the Creator. These traditions teach that certain plants have entered into a holy pact with humans: they will give their lives so that people

may have the sacred smoke with which to cleanse themselves; in return, we must treat these plants with respect, asking permission to pick them, giving thanks for their sacrifice, taking only what we need, and leaving the plant as undamaged as possible.

The use of sacred smoke in purification rites, however, is not limited to Native Americans. First Peoples from around the globe have historically used burning herbs or incense in ceremony and ritual. In India, for instance, sandalwood has been burned for centuries as an aid to meditation. Celtic and Germanic peoples cleansed themselves in the fragrant smoke from herbal mixtures thrown on hot rocks or into the fire in their sweat lodges. Indeed, even the wafting of incense in the Christian Mass can be seen as a form of smudging.

Smudging can be used for minor healing, for balancing energy, or for fostering a state of calmness or centeredness. People who are suffering from relationship problems or are in a state of grieving or anxiety can often find peace of mind from a simple smudging ceremony.

Smudging is also used to cleanse ritual objects, such as those used in healing ceremonies, though reports of decrepit autos and balky computers being 'cured' by smudge smoke abound.

Smudging is also a powerful tool for clearing your home or office of negative influences, either to banish the energies of previous inhabitants when you first move in, or to rid the space of 'bad vibes' created by unpleasant or painful events. See pages 34–37 for how to perform a Smudge Ceremony at home.

The feng shui belief that, by clearing out the clutter in your home, you are clearing out the clutter in your life is similar to the concept of sympathetic magic, the basis of much spell craft in nature magic.

Sympathetic magic means using a symbol or symbolic action to help focus on what you want to achieve. For example, for a drought-breaking spell, a native tribe might throw pebbles onto the roofs of its huts to symbolize and encourage the return of rain.

A broom can also be used in this way. Wielding it to sweep away dust symbolizes sweeping away the intangible negative psychic energy that has accumulated in spaces where traumas have been experienced or intense emotions such as anger have been expressed.

As with feng shui, nature magic uses sounds to drive away negative energy from a room, a house, or a special space. A nature magic spell to clear a space may consist of chanting a simple phrase and using products of the earth, such as salt, herbs, essential oils and candles.

CLEANSING AND PURIFYING

Salt is the principal ingredient used in nature magic for cleansing and purifying a space. Its cleansing properties have been known for centuries. You can sprinkle it directly on the ground around your house; however, if sprinkling pure salt would damage your lawn, you could dilute it in purified or distilled water. The solution may also be splashed around each opening in the house, or sprayed using a plant mister.

In nature magic, any cleansing is done from within a circle. The circle is created either physically, by drawing a line in the earth around your space, or mentally, by imagining a line of blue or light purple light curving around to form your space. As a precaution, always 'cast' (draw or imagine) a circle around yourself when dealing with strong negative energies.

Lit candles, semiprecious stones and herbs are used in nature magic practices to enhance the energy within the space. To purify and protect a space, white or natural-colored candles made from natural substances such as beeswax or palm oil are usually used. Candles of specific colors can be lit to attract a certain type of energy to your home — for example, a red or pink candle for love and friendship or a green candle for money.

If you want to fulfill your desire to attract love or financial abundance, many nature magic practices require you to visualize strongly the success of your wish. You will need to 'anchor' a mental image of the spell's outcome, such as yourself looking relaxed and happy, to your candle, semiprecious stone or herb. This will make the outcome and the object one. See page 33 for herbs used for protection and cleansing.

THE ELEMENTS:
OBSERVING THE NATURAL WORLD AROUND YOU

In Chinese philosophy, there are five elements or forces of nature — water, wood, fire, earth and metal. Their constant state of movement contributes to the creation of qi, the universal energy force. In feng shui the number five is considered very lucky, because of the belief about the five elements. (In many Western magical practices, four is a lucky, balanced number, whereas in feng shui four is believed to augur death, because the word for death in Chinese sounds very much like the word for this number.)

Two types of cycles involve the elements — a productive cycle and a destructive one. The productive cycle generates beneficial qi, and is linked to the flow of the seasons. Each Chinese element represents one of five seasons in the Chinese calendar.

THE ELEMENTS AND THE SEASONS

Winter is a water element. The next season is spring, which is a wood element. Water nourishes wood and is part of the productive cycle. Summer is fire, which is fed by the wood of spring, while earth represents the energy of the Chinese season of late summer, a short period of six weeks in which it is believed that the earth is experiencing a supreme balance between dark and light, life and death. Autumn is represented by metal, which is contained in the earth and can, when made into a vessel, contain water, the element linked to winter.

THE DESTRUCTIVE CYCLE IN THE HOME

The destructive cycle generates negative energy. In the home, negative energy will be present in a room that contains two conflicting elements. For example, the kitchen contains the potentially destructive quality of both water (the sink for washing up) and fire (the stove).

If the following elements are placed in the same room, tension will result:

- metal and wood *(think of an axe chopping down a tree)*
- wood and earth *(think of a tree taking energy out of the ground)*
- earth and water *(think of earth thrown into water, making mud)*
- water and fire *(think of a bucket of water putting out a fire)*
- fire and metal *(think of a furnace melting down metal).*

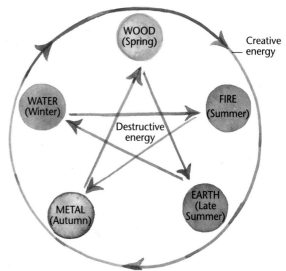

The arrows around the circle show the productive flow of energy between the elements representing the seasons. The arrows within the circle link the elements that generate negative energy when placed together.

NATURE MAGIC ELEMENTS

As in feng shui with its fundamental elements, nature magic also venerates elements — earth, air, fire and water — as the essential elements of the world. A fifth element, spirit, is often also counted; it is considered as either the result of the combination of the four elements, or the representation of the cosmos.

SPACE CLEARING AND THE ELEMENTS

If you feel tension in your home, check the combination of elements. Check if your rooms contain elements such as a water feature directly opposite the mouth of your chimney. Or look outside for an element that may be disruptive — for example, a metal chimney across from your wooden decking. Remove any objects that could symbolize a destructive element combination, and see if this helps clear feelings of negativity.

YOUR TOOLS FOR CLEARING YOUR SPACE

For feng shui clearing you will need a compass, a grid and a house plan. These are used to work out which area of your house matches which aspiration of your life (see pages 12–13). To prepare your house plan, draw a rough plan of your house and its interior. Mark out the rooms and the placement of your furniture, and then all the spots where clutter congregates. Note on your plan approximately what is accumulating in these areas. This plan will be one of your major tools for clearing your home and the corresponding aspects of your life.

For the grid, draw a square or rectangle around the outside walls of your house and subdivide it into nine equal sections. The wall containing the front door or the main entrance to your house will form the bottom line of the grid. Label each section as below:

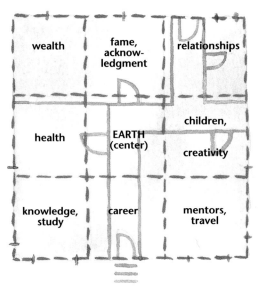

Remember that the bottom of the grid should be lined up with the wall that contains the main entrance to your space. You can also do this grid for a single room.

Use the suggestions in this book to clear the clutter from the various areas of your home you have marked. Work on one area at a time. If you see that a particular area in your house or space corresponds with an aspect of your life you are finding troublesome at the moment, clear that area first. Then observe how the cleansing effect helps you in your life.

Many tools exist to help you clear your space, cleansing and enhancing the energy of your house. They include sound, smoke, scent, candles, semiprecious stones, herbs and symbols.

SOUND

You might choose one of the following tools to let sound clear your space:

- five-rod wind chimes
- gongs
- drums (the Irish bodhrán, which is shaped like a tambourine and is hit with a stick, is a favorite with nature magic practitioners)
- Tibetan cymbals
- crystal singing bowls.

You may also clear space by making your own sounds: chant a mantra (a repeated phrase), clap your hands, or do a toning session. Toning is a technique that enables you to make sustained sounds of deep quality. Recordings of chants, tonings and music for meditation are available commercially. Music suggestions are given on page 68.

AROMA

One of the most effective ways of clearing negative energies from your space is to use a smudge stick made of sage (see page 34). Sage has an antiseptic and astringent quality, and has been used for centuries by the North American Indians to clear spaces of negative energies. The herb can also be used to clear the mind and encourage rational thought processes. There are also special Chinese clearing incenses and certain essential oils, such as lemon, which stimulate the flow of qi. Herbs for protection are listed on page 33.

YOU AND THE ENVIRONMENT: DISPERSING NEGATIVE ENERGY

In feng shui, it is important to disperse negative energy. One way of doing so in your home is by using the nature magic practice of grounding the energy. Hold a piece of rock, semiprecious stone or clear quartz crystal, and visualize the negative energy pouring from the atmosphere around you into this object. Then take the stone outside and push it into the ground to symbolize the return of the energy to the earth for cleansing and renewal. Do this exercise only when you have also done a grounding exercise (see pages 62–63).

Humans can tap into the earth's energy. Doing this is one of the main ways of harnessing the energy required for powering nature magic spells. Be aware that certain places have a stronger build-up of energy than is usual for residential areas. These high-energy places are usually sites that have been devoted to worship for centuries, or that contain natural phenomena with high energy levels — volcanoes, earthquake zones and so on.

Ley lines are lines drawn between such sites. They are thought to correspond with important paths or pilgrimage trails of spiritual significance, and to give us an understanding of the earth's energy fields. Where seven or more ley lines intersect, a ley center is created. Ley centers are believed to have a particularly powerful build-up of psychic energy. Such ley centers include the English sites of Glastonbury Tor and Stonehenge.

Feng shui practitioners advise that we avoid living near places of strong energy, because the excess of energy can be either too yin (introspective), in the case of churches, ancient burial sites and cemeteries, or too yang (expansive), in the case of volcanoes and earthquake zones. They also advise avoiding human-made concentrations of energy such as electricity sources. Accordingly, living under electrical lines or next to electrical substations should be avoided. Your electricity supply should not share the same wall as a bed, as this may cause sleep disturbances, problematic behavior and a propensity for ill health.

Feng shui practitioners also focus on the electromagnetic fields created by electrical appliances used in the home. They suggest limiting exposure to television, computers, and even clock radios (see pages 38–39). Sometimes appliances such as stereo systems can be used in certain areas to stimulate the flow of qi. Often, however, practitioners advise throwing a cloth over appliances, or turning them off when not in use to minimize emissions. It is a good idea to also place appliances away in a cupboard or storage area when not in use, to reduce clutter.

Clearing Your Home

The power of Feng Shui in Your Home

If your whole house, or one of your rooms, is causing you discomfort, or your luck seems to have hit rock bottom, you must be surrounded by stagnant energy. Fortunately, there are some very simple things you can do to clear it away.

First, stand at your front door or the door leading into the unsettled room in your house. Qi, or universal energy, enters your house or room through this door. Make a note of what you see and feel. Is there a straight path leading to the door — for example, a straight garden path or a corridor? If so, this means that the energy is flowing too quickly into the house or room. Place some wind chimes or a potted plant with rounded leaves somewhere along the path of the energy. Try this for three days, and see if the energy in the house or room feels clearer.

Second, check if there are any sharp angles pointing directly at your front door. For example, outside your house a sharp angle may be caused by a pole with electricity lines, the angle of a neighbor's roof, or a road leading directly to your door. Inside the house, a sharp angle may be formed by a staircase banister or a corner where two walls meet. To counter a sharp angle inside your house, place a wind chime, a red or gold tassel or a plant between the door and the angle. If there is a sharp line directed at your front door or at one of the windows of the

A bagua mirror will deflect poison arrows from your front door.

HOW TO TELL IF THE ENERGY HAS CLEARED

If you feel that the energy has cleared, don't think you are merely reacting to suggestion. Trust your senses. You need to realize, given the chance, your intuition can be both powerful and perceptive. Here are some indications that the negative energy has been cleared. You may feel that:

•

there is a lightness in the air

•

the colors in the room or house are brighter

•

everything is in its place

•

an indefinable worry is no longer lingering around you

affected room, place a mirror (either a bagua mirror or a simple convex mirror) outside, directly in line with the sharp point. Try this for three days, and see if the energy in the house or room feels clearer.

You can also use nature magic practices to break the negative energy coming into your space. Plant a protective tree, such as the rowan or European mountain ash, between the fixture generating a poison arrow and your front door. Also consider planting protective herbs such as basil or dill in a window box to break the path of the flow of negative energy into your home.

THE ANCIENT TRADITION OF 'HOUSEWARMINGS': MOVING INTO A NEW PLACE

Before you buy or rent a home or workplace, feng shui practitioners would advise you to ask about the former residents. Why are they leaving the premises? Have they experienced a relationship breakup? Have they had to downsize their business?

If the premises become available because their occupiers have come into money and bought a bigger home, or because the occupiers' business has expanded and bigger premises are needed, there is a great chance that this space has a good flow of energy. If residents are moving for different reasons, however, reconsider moving in. But if you do have to continue with the purchase or agreement to rent, don't be concerned. There are a number of ways you can cleanse the accumulated negative energy from the space and attract a better flow of energy into your home life or business.

It is important to start by cleansing the area physically. Have all surfaces washed and all carpets cleaned. Consider repainting and even changing the carpet. Look at buying plants and using fabrics made from natural fibers. Also consider holding a housewarming party (for tips about an office-warming ceremony, see pages 64–65).

The term 'housewarming' comes from the ancient Roman and Greek traditions of transferring glowing embers from the hearth of a family's old home to the hearth of their new one. This practice stems from the belief that the spirits protecting the house live in the hearth. These household spirits were thought to be in charge of the family's luck and sustenance. If the glowing embers were moved, the spirits could continue protecting the family.

Therefore, to introduce personal, positive energies into your new home or workplace, you should have a housewarming party after you have neutralized your space by cleaning it. Consider asking your friends to bring a personal blessing for you. Get them to write down their good wishes on paper. Then, during the party, light your hearth, burn all the papers with sage, and fan the smoke around the house. If you do not have a hearth, use a large metal bowl half filled with sand. Burn the papers in a small pile in the middle with a sprinkling of sage over the top.

Alternatively, consider doing a smudging (see pages 14–15 and 34–37) during your housewarming party, inviting your friends to participate in visualizing a happy future for you in your new space.

DISPELLING CLUTTER AND DUST:
SPRING CLEANING YOUR LIFE

Spring is one of the traditional times for renewing your energies and those of your home. The increase in the sun's energy at this time of year is reflected in a feeling of increased creativity and an interest in exploring new activities. By removing clutter and the stale energy of winter from the house, you are creating space for a new energy to come in and revitalize you and your family. Doing so will make you feel linked with the energies of the season.

If you are using feng shui principles, you do not have to wait until spring to clean your space. In the Tong Shu, the feng shui almanac of lucky and unlucky days, there are specific days designated for housecleaning which are usually spaced two weeks apart. If you don't have access to the Tong Shu consider, as a general rule, dusting and removing clutter from your space on a day that suits you once every two weeks.

If you are feeling unfocused, aimless or in a rut, consider removing clutter from your premises. Often the amassing of a lot of material objects is an indication of stagnation. This stagnation may be a sign that you are unhappy with your life and that you are using the clutter around you as a barricade.

If you don't know where to start to unclutter your space, stand at your front door and look at the interior of your house. Can you see a clutter of books, papers, furniture or objects from the front door? This is the first area you will need to tidy up, because it is the first obstacle placed in the path of the qi energy's movement through your house. Alternatively, you could begin by tidying up the area that corresponds to a problem in your life (see page 20 for how to use your feng shui house plan).

Clearing clutter takes time. You will need to sort through what has been accumulated and work out whether you want to keep it or throw it out. If you do need to keep some of your things, consider whether storage will be a problem. If you have no time to clear the space but would like to start the clearing process, try placing or hanging a clear quartz crystal on the pile of clutter. Wash the crystal in some running water before positioning it. The crystal will attract positive energy to the space, and will also encourage you to come into it to start clearing up.

(see page 20 for how to use your feng shui house plan).

STARTING TO CLEAR THE CLUTTER

TIP: Begin by giving yourself a small uncluttering task that you know you will be able to complete within a short time. For example, clear the clutter from a coffee table, bookshelf or an untidy drawer of your study desk or dressing table. Don't try to unclutter your whole house in one go. If you start too big a job, you may feel overwhelmed, creating an even bigger mess than the one you had started with. When clearing your selected area, ask yourself what is the worst thing that could happen if you throw an item away. If the item is not necessary to you at the moment, let it go by throwing it or giving it away.

~

The sense of achievement you will feel by uncluttering even a small space will evoke an increased feeling of order and control that will ease stress. Since clutter can be an indication of an attachment to the past or a fear of the future, as you progressively tidy each small space, you will find a new sense of serenity and freedom from chaos. You will also find that the more space you create within your environment, the more space you will have in your life to consider new opportunities and fresh beginnings.

REMOVING NEGATIVE ENERGY WITH FENG SHUI

If you or your family, your workforce or previous house owners or tenants have experienced anger, trauma or sustained unhappiness in a space, these emotions will be 'encoded' into the energy fields within the premises. To expel this negative energy, consider requesting a feng shui practitioner with space clearing experience to help remove the negative energy left by these strong experiences. Alternatively, you may wish to carry out the following simple ritual yourself.

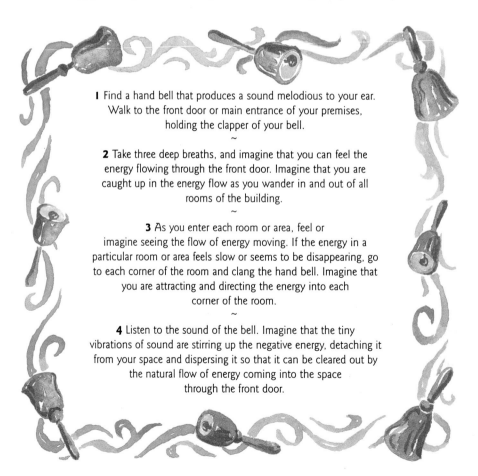

I Find a hand bell that produces a sound melodious to your ear. Walk to the front door or main entrance of your premises, holding the clapper of your bell.

~

2 Take three deep breaths, and imagine that you can feel the energy flowing through the front door. Imagine that you are caught up in the energy flow as you wander in and out of all rooms of the building.

~

3 As you enter each room or area, feel or imagine seeing the flow of energy moving. If the energy in a particular room or area feels slow or seems to be disappearing, go to each corner of the room and clang the hand bell. Imagine that you are attracting and directing the energy into each corner of the room.

~

4 Listen to the sound of the bell. Imagine that the tiny vibrations of sound are stirring up the negative energy, detaching it from your space and dispersing it so that it can be cleared out by the natural flow of energy coming into the space through the front door.

Be aware that, when these encoded energies are released, you may briefly experience an echo of the negative emotions or of the unhappy person's spirit. Remember that this is an echo only, and is not part of your current existence, even though the energy may still be intruding on your life. Anyone doing space clearing, practitioner or layperson alike, could wear a small feng shui charm such as a jade Bi as protection from any stray negativity. This charm is a round piece of jade with a hole in the middle. It may contain a coin or a Chinese good luck character. After the space clearing, you could hang the jade charm on the back of your front door to continue protecting your space from negative energy.

HOW TO STOP GOOD LUCK FROM LEAKING OUT OF YOUR HOME

Fix leaking taps promptly.

•

Always flush your toilet with the lid down.

•

Place a sink plug in all sink drain holes.

•

Cover all floor drain holes with natural fabric until they are needed.

•

Always keep the laundry and bathroom doors closed.

Both feng shui and nature magic offer many ways of protecting your house. In feng shui, energy stagnation and poison arrows can create areas in your house or building that not only feel uncomfortable, but that also attract bad luck, particularly in the form of break-ins and burglaries. In nature magic, a similar concept applies, based on the premise that negative energy attracts negative energy.

All nature magic rituals for cleansing and placing a protection around your house require you to concentrate first on being protected yourself. The first step is to take a bath before the cleansing and protection ritual, to wash away the worries of the day. This will help you focus all your concentration on the purpose of the ritual. Then you can imagine that you are protected in a blue or purple cocoon of light.

Once the space is cleansed (clearing through nature magic is discussed on pages 16–17), consider carrying out the protection ritual.

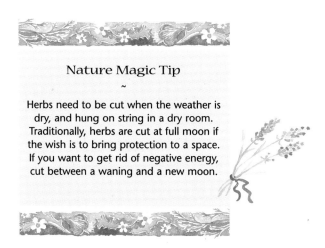

Nature Magic Tip

~

Herbs need to be cut when the weather is dry, and hung on string in a dry room. Traditionally, herbs are cut at full moon if the wish is to bring protection to a space. If you want to get rid of negative energy, cut between a waning and a new moon.

After bathing, and after visualizing that you are being protected, you may wish to protect all of the openings to the house by one of the following methods:

1 Sprinkle salt lightly on all windowsills and the front and back doorsteps. As you are sprinkling the salt, visualize that each grain is protecting the house from harm.

2 Grow or buy fennel, St John's Wort or another herb known for its protective qualities (see the table of herbs below), and tie your chosen herbs together in neat small bundles using braided strands of red cotton or wool thread. Prepare one bundle for each entry door and each window in your space. At the new moon, hang a bundle over each doorway and window. Leave the herbs to hang for a full cycle of the moon.

3 Grow protective herbs (select from the table below) at your front and back doorsteps.

4 Place a magically charged talisman at the front and back doorsteps. Place it under a mat or potted plant, or bury it in the soil near the doorsteps.

5 Hang some turquoise beads on the inside of your front and back doors.

Herb	Properties
Chamomile	Calms and protects
Dill	Dispels negative energies
Fennel	Protects, enhances ability to face danger and adversity
Garlic	Protects, gives strength
Ginger	Protects
Hyssop	Protects, particularly the house
Sage	Gives wisdom, cleanses evil
Valerian	Protects and cleanses

SMUDGING PLANTS

North American Indians employed four plants in particular in their smudging ceremonies, either alone or in combination.

SAGE   The sage used by Native Americans in smudging ceremonies is not the cooking herb, but rather the sagebrush that graces Western movies, of the genus Artemisia. Three varieties of the Artemisia genus that grow in North America are *A. californica*, or common sagebrush, *A. vulgaris*, or mugwort, and *A. tridentata*, native to the Great Plains and the Rocky Mountains. All are woody plants, ideal for burning in bundles, and can be used interchangeably. Sage is traditionally burned to drive out ill feelings or influences, negative energies, and evil entities, and to protect the sacred space where ceremonies will take place. Smudging with sage provides clarity and reduces stress, while freeing spaces from psychic noise.

CEDAR   Both the dried needles and wood shavings of Western Red Cedar *(Thuja occidentalis)* and California Incense Cedar *(Libocedrus descurrens)* prove ideal for smudging. Cedar is burned to cleanse a house before moving in, particularly in the Northwest and Western Canadian traditions, and to carry prayers to the Creator. The smoke from cedar promotes balance and harmony, and so is particularly effective for preparing our living and working spaces. Cedar needles are also used to bring balance to the male/female elements.

SWEETGRASS   One of the most important plants to First Nations People, sweetgrass *(Hierochloe oderanta)* is frequently burned after sage and/or cedar to invite in benevolent influences. Also known as Mother Earth's hair, holy grass, seneca grass, and vanilla grass, it is braided like a hair plait at harvest time, with the whole strand often burned for smudging. Its sweet smoke is believed to lift the spirits of the downhearted, banish negative thoughts and emotions, unite the people in a sacred circle, and bring sweetness and light into our lives. Sweetgrass is rare and hard to come by today, so perhaps using a less endangered plant such as lavender would be more in keeping with the sacred purpose of a smudging ritual.

TOBACCO   Tobacco is considered a sacred plant, credited with linking the earth with the spirit world, and used to carry prayers to the Creator and for making offerings. If you wish to use tobacco in a ceremonial manner, avoid pipe, cigar, and cigarette tobaccos, as these are usually polluted with highly toxic chemicals. If you do manage to find an organic tobacco leaf, use it only in smudging ceremonies performed outside.

Many other herbs from different cultures are used in modern smudging ceremonies. If you are not following a particular tradition, experiment with various combinations until you find ones that suit you and your own particular background. Following are just some of the herbs and gum resins to consider.

LAVENDER	Popular as an aromatherapy herb, lavender calms and relaxes, and promotes harmony and forgiveness. Consider substituting its sweetly fragrant smoke in place of sweetgrass for calling in positive energy.
GARDEN AND WHITE SAGES	*Salvia officinalis* and *Salvia apiana,* the herbs used in cooking, are excellent for smudging because of their healing properties. Indeed, the genus name Salvia is derived from the Latin word *salvare,* which means 'to heal' or 'to save'.
OREGANO AND THYME	The aromatic oils of these cooking herbs have antiseptic and anti-viral properties, making oregano and thyme appropriate herbs for use in healing ceremonies.
JUNIPER AND PIÑON PINE	Similar in effect to cedar, juniper and piñon pine provide balance and harmony, inviting in beneficent energy.
SANDALWOOD	The aromatic smoke of sandalwood helps establish a meditative state.
AMBER	A fossilized resin, amber is said to connect us to ancient wisdom.
COPAL	Native to South and Central America, copal was used by the Aztecs in purification and cleansing rituals.

Smudge mixes are easily obtainable, either over the Internet, or at stores that specialize in Native American crafts. You can also grow or gather many of the plants yourself.

PREPARATION

At its simplest, smudging requires no more than a bundle of dried herbs tied with twine, a match, and the proper attitude. You should approach the smudging ceremony in a spirit of love and openness. Banish negative thoughts and energies as you enter ceremonial space. Deep, rhythmic breathing can help you to become calm and centered, and to connect to the here and now. Focus on the purpose of the ritual, leaving your everyday concerns and worries behind.

THE SMUDGING CEREMONY

No single 'right' way to smudge exists. However, investing the smudging with a sense of ritual might help you to better concentrate on the reason you are performing a smudging in the first place. Here is a smudging ceremony that you can use as a template. Change details as your intuition and preferences move you.

Fill a smudge pot (which can be purchased at a Native American crafts store or a new age store), a fireproof bowl, or a clam or abalone shell with

MATERIALS NEEDED

- Smudge mixture or bundle of dried herbs
- An earthenware or fireproof dish or shell filled with sand, or a smudge pot, or a small brazier
- Mesquite charcoal briquette, or small piece of charcoal from a fire (do not use charcoal impregnated with lighter fluid!)
- A lighter or match
- A feather or fan

sand. Some traditions will not use shells, as they believe that the water element nullifies the fire element. Others feel that the shell brings balance, adding the fourth element water to the earth, air, and fire already present in the ceremony. You may feel that you would like to use only a bundle of herbs, with no container whatsoever.

If using a bundle of herbs, you can stick the stems in the sand, then light the leafy part. Put the fire out by waving your feather or fan over the herbs (blowing the flame out is considered ill-advised, as breathing on the herbs can add your own negative energy to the mix).

Gum resins (such as copal or sandalwood), powdered smudging mixtures, and wood shavings and needles should be burned on a mesquite or hardwood charcoal briquette. Place the briquette in a small brazier or fireproof vessel filled with sand. Light one corner of the charcoal. You can fan the briquette with your feather or fan. Then, sprinkle some of the smudging material on to the charcoal.

If you are performing the smudging ceremony alone, you should first smudge yourself. If other participants are involved, you can take turns smudging one another.

Offer some smoke to the four directions, starting with east, and then smudge downwards and upwards to Mother Earth and Father Sky. Bring the smudge near to your heart. Then, starting with your left leg (left representing the receiving side of your body), draw the smudge up along your body, using your feather or fan to waft the smoke both in front and in back of you. Fan the smoke upward, as Father Sky is strong enough to absorb the negative energy you are banishing. Continue down your right side (right being the giving side of your body), this time wafting the smoke downwards towards Mother Earth. Concentrate the smoke on any parts of your body that hurt or need healing.

After you have smudged yourself, you may bathe any objects needing smudging in the herbal smoke. If you are smudging your home, start outdoors on the east side and walk around the building clockwise, fanning the smoke towards the house. Next, enter your house, being sure all the windows and doors are open. Again, starting on the east side, walk clockwise through the house, filling every corner with the smudge smoke. Use your feather or fan to waft the smoke, carrying all the negative energy and any malevolent influences out of the house. A variation of this practice may be used for a room only, or for your office or place of business.

Focus on the present, keeping your breathing deep and steady. Ask for help and healing. When you have finished, let the herbs cool, then return them to the Earth with reverence. Finish the smudging by thanking the plants for their sacrifice.

CLEARING YOUR PERSONAL SPACE: THE BEDROOM

GETTING A BETTER NIGHT'S SLEEP: REMOVING CLUTTER

Your bedroom is one of the most important areas to keep clear of clutter and disruptive energies. It is your personal sanctuary, and represents in miniature who you are and what is happening in your life. The placement of furniture, pictures and electrical equipment can have a particularly strong effect on both your emotional life and your health.

According to feng shui principles, if you sleep poorly there are three main things you should consider doing to help create a peaceful atmosphere:

1 Clear the space under your bed. Do not have any storage there. In feng shui, having clutter under your bed means you are sleeping on all the issues you do not want to face. This will lead to many nights of disturbed sleep.

2 Keep electrical appliances to a minimum. If you have a television set or radio in your bedroom, consider moving it out of the room altogether, or keep it covered with an attractive 'yin'-colored cloth. Yin colors include dark greens, blues and purples. Clock radios are also frowned upon.

3 Cover any mirrors in your bedroom. In feng shui, it is believed that your spirit rises as you sleep, and will be disturbed by seeing itself in a mirror. Having no mirrors in the bedroom, or covering up any mirrors present, is also considered an important factor for rectifying an unhappy relationship or marriage.

Removing clutter also means keeping the top of your dressing table clear of unused or empty bottles, your hair brushes and hand mirrors clean, your chest of drawers tidy and your clothing freshly laundered and in good repair.

Your closet or wardrobe should be similarly maintained. Throw out or give away all clothes that no longer fit you. Consider separating out the ones that remain into wear for the different seasons. Then store the clothes that will not be needed for a few months in a closet or wardrobe that is close to a steady flow of energy. Do not store too many things in your bedroom.

The position of your bed is also very important. Check that it is not placed under a beam. People sleeping under beams have been found to suffer from stabbing pains, and from illnesses arising from constrictions in the area where the beam crosses the body. For example, if the beam is right above your head, you may experience headaches or migraines. Also check that the bed is not in the 'coffin position', that is, with the footboard pointing directly out of the bedroom door.

You may also consider moving your bed to face your favorable direction. Check the chart on pages 78–79. It specifies, according to the year in which you were born, which direction you should face in your bed if you want to have a good night's sleep and attract good luck and fortune.

FENG SHUI TIP

If you have a bedroom clock with a digital display, try to keep it at least 3 feet (1 meter) away from your head to reduce exposure to electromagnetic radiation. If your clock is electronic, it is best to run it on a battery rather than having it connected to the external electricity supply.

CLEANSING UNHAPPINESS FROM YOUR LIFE

Your bedroom is your personal space, and is an intimate reflection of your life. Feng shui practitioners believe that a cluttered bedroom is an indication of disorganization and a lack of focus, particularly within your personal relationships.

Your bedroom may be the only room in the house where you can easily move furniture around, remove clutter and perform some cleansing rituals. Also, since the bedroom is a smaller area to organize than the whole house, rearranging it is an excellent first step to clearing clutter from your life.

If you have a general feeling of unhappiness with the direction of your life, stand at the main entrance of your bedroom — the doorway — and examine where you can see clutter and disorganization. Use the feng shui house plan described on pages 20–21 for your bedroom alone, aligning the plan with the wall that contains your doorway.

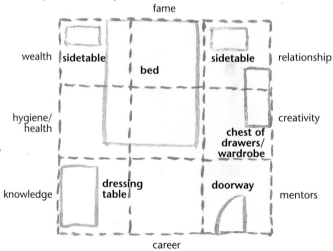

Mark on your plan where the clutter has congregated. What does it consist of — bedclothes, clothing, cosmetics? Make a note of what is cluttering up each area. Sometimes the nature of the clutter can symbolize what you are feeling about

FENG SHUI TIP

When moving into a new house, always purchase new pillows. This means a new beginning, and symbolizes that you are leaving your old problems behind you.

your life. For example, a stash of empty or near-empty perfume and cosmetics bottles or jars on a dressing table may be cluttering your relationships corner. In feng shui, it is believed that clearing all empty bottles and replenishing your supplies will dispel feelings of loneliness or emptiness in your life.

The first step to cleansing your space of unhappiness is to clear the area of all clutter. Clear your bedroom totally of unnecessary objects, tidy all your clothes, change your bedclothes and make up the bed afresh. Then, consulting your house plan, ring a hand bell over all areas where the clutter has accumulated. Pay particular attention to your bed, ringing the bell over every inch of it. Give special focus to the pillows — this is a very useful ritual if you have marital problems, or if you or your spouse or partner are suffering sleep problems.

As part of the bed often lies in the center of the bedroom, ensure that you always make it, and keep the bedclothes fresh and clean. Feng shui practitioners believe that the center of the house or room corresponds with the earth element, and the state it is in is a general indication of the flow of energy in the premises, or in the person's life. So if you keep the center of your bedroom tidy, you will find that your life will flow smoothly and feel less troubled.

Never position your bed directly in the center of the room, because this may cause you feelings of anxiety and nervousness. The best position for your bed is to have either the headboard or the side of the bed against the wall in your favorable direction (see pages 78–79).

Nature Magic Tip

~

On the day of a new moon, air your pillows in the sun until they smell fresh and clean. Take them into the house during the twilight hours and then let them lie in a place where they are in full view of the new moon. This will help clear the build-up of psychic energies that are experienced during sleep.

ENHANCING YOUR PROSPECTS OF NEW LOVE

One of the possible benefits of clearing and cleansing the space in the bedroom area is that these actions may make this space more conducive to attracting positive energy, and even love.

Before attempting to enhance your prospects of new love, you should follow the suggestions given in this chapter for generally clearing your bedroom. Once you have cleared all negative energies by getting rid of the clutter and tidying up your bed and closet or wardrobe, you will be able to enhance particular areas of your life by redecorating corresponding areas of your bedroom. If you want to enhance your prospects of love, you will need to work on the relationship corner (see the grid on page 40).

To attract a new love, or to rekindle the flame of your existing relationship, follow these simple tips for decorating a bedroom:

1 Remove all pictures of yourself in which you are on your own.
2 Remove all empty jars and bottles.
3 Remove all pictures of, and objects given by, past partners in unhappy relationships.
4 Make sure there are even numbers of decorative objects such as candles, side tables and pictures.
5 If you are buying furniture for your bedroom, consider dressing tables and chests of drawers that have even numbers of drawers.
6 Include special feng shui good-luck symbols for love, such as a pair of ducks or an open red fan.

Some special objects may be placed directly in the relationship corner of your bedroom (see page 40). Once you have located this corner, use a hand bell, or just clap your hands loudly in it to make sure that the area is clear of negative energy. Try to organize your furniture so that there is a flat surface in this corner that can be made into a small space devoted to attracting a relationship or enhancing your current relationship.

In this space, you could place a combination of the following to improve your prospects for love:

- two pieces of rose quartz of equal size
- a yang-colored cloth (yang colors include red, orange and pink)
- a pair of red candles
- images of butterflies (not actual dead butterflies).

You may also wish to include a pair of objects that symbolize the element with which you correspond (see the table below). In feng shui, it is believed that each person's energy corresponds with one of the five Chinese elements — fire, air, water, metal or wood. To find out your element, check the chart on pages 78–79, which lists the elements according to a person's year of birth within the Chinese solar year.

Element	Suggestions for objects corresponding with your element
Earth	Ceramic cups
Metal	Metal-framed picture of a couple
Wood	Wooden-framed picture of a couple
Water	Two glasses of water
Fire	Two red candles

CLEARING YOUR FAMILY SPACE: THE LIVING ROOM

WHEN THE ARGUMENTS GET TOO MUCH: CLEARING THE AIR

Are there too many arguments in your family? If so, both feng shui and nature magic offer a number of ways to effectively lower feelings of aggression among family members.

During an argument, one of the hardest tasks is listening rather than talking louder than the others involved. You can alleviate feelings of resentment by making sure that neither you nor other family members are standing or sitting with backs to a doorway. If you are in the living room, make sure that there is an even number of chairs, and that you and your family are all sitting in a position where you can see the doorway. This will lead all of you to seek — and find — solutions to your problems.

Make a note of where the arguments erupt in your home and your workplace. Check that these areas are not at the end of a long corridor — a spot that suffers from hard-hitting 'poison arrows' generated by fast moving qi. Check also that the living room is not being struck by 'poison arrows' made by sharp lines from a neighbor's roof line. If it is, implement the solutions discussed on pages 24–25.

Take note as well of the subject matter of the pictures decorating the walls of your living area. Are they harmonious? Do they have pleasant associations? If not, replace the offending pictures, because they are symbolic of the current feelings of the family.

Once you have implemented a cure, ring a melodious hand bell in the area. Constant arguments make the air of an area feel heavy, sound flat and seem dull in color (as if the area is covered in a light layer of dust). Ring the bell over the area, particularly over upholstered pieces of furniture, until you sense a change in the air. Upholstery can soak up a lot of negative energy because it has close contact with people. Burn a stick of lavender incense to further help clear the air of aggression, and to instill a calming atmosphere that will cling to or permeate any natural fabrics in the room.

If you are having continual arguments with a troubled child, check to see what compass direction the child is facing while sleeping or studying. Check the table on pages 78–79 for the child's favorable compass direction, and experiment with moving his or her bed or desk to face the direction listed in the table. Also remove mirrors from your child's bedroom, or cover them, as it is believed that mirrors reflect your image while you are sleeping, making your spirit feel uneasy. Mirrors also reflect light, creating an energy in the bedroom that is too strong.

If doors are banged in anger by your child, you can use a special 'feng shui ring bell charm' on his or her door to encourage their co-operation. The charm is a small bell hanging within a ring. The ring is covered with a knotted cord that ends in a tassel, and the charm can be hung on the inside of the door to your child's bedroom or the front door by a decorative looped cord that is attached to the ring.

The banging of doors may also symbolize the attempts of your children to attract more energy so that it will flow to them. Make sure that the doors in your house (particularly the front door) do not stick or creak, as this is an indication that energy is not flowing properly through the house.

CLEANSING YOUR SPACE FOR NEW FRIENDS

To attract new friends and mentors into your life, concentrate on clearing out all the clutter in the area of your house, workplace, room or desk that corresponds to the mentor aspiration. Use the feng shui house plan for your space (see page 20), aligning it with the wall that contains the main doorway into the area.

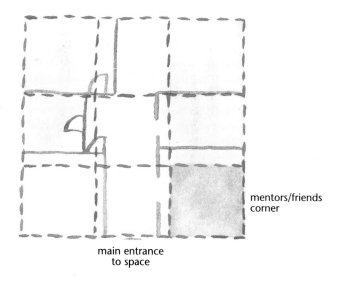

mentors/friends
corner

main entrance
to space

If you wish to attract new friends to your family in general, concentrate on clearing the corresponding area of your home. If this space lies in a private space, for example, one of the children's bedrooms, consider creating a small 'altar' in one of the public rooms, such as the family room, to attract friends and helpful people to you and your family.

To do this, place the above grid over a plan of the room chosen, such as the family room, aligning the bottom of the grid with the wall that contains the main entrance into the room. This entrance will be the one through which you would enter the room as you walk from the front door. Keep this area clear of clutter.

To make an altar to attract good friends, put together some pictures of yourself and your friends in this area, as well as objects that remind you of your friends. Also include some lucky feng shui objects to attract friends and mentors, such as an image or statue of an elephant.

Follow the practice of checking the chosen area for any poison arrows directed to the room from poles outside or from the corners of internal walls, and implement cures to block any fast-flowing shafts of energy. Ring a melodious hand bell in the area until you sense a difference. If you do not have a hand bell, try clapping in the corners where stagnant energy can build up, and also clap over upholstered chairs, sofas and cushions.

Once the space feels clear, hang a wind chime in a corner of it to increase the possibility of making new friends. Other sounds can also be included in this area, which is an excellent place for your stereo system. However, when you are playing music on your stereo, make sure the sound is not too loud. Loud sounds over-stimulate energy, changing it from a balanced to an aggressive energy.

Introduce more light into this area by hanging a faceted crystal in one of the windows, or keeping a lamp switched on during the day or night (use a lower wattage bulb to conserve energy). Include mirrors as well, to reflect the light already coming into the area. Align a mirror on a wall so that it reflects a pleasant arrangement within the room or a view outside your window.

WAYS OF ATTRACTING FRIENDSHIP

If you feel unworthy of attracting new, compatible friends, nature magic can be used to improve your feelings about this. A stone placed in the mentor/friendship area of your bedroom can help you to find the assurance lost through past hurts. Of all stones, minerals and ores, the following are particularly useful for encouraging friendships:

- barite (promotes self-assurance and enhances friendships)
- manganese (strengthens bonds and feelings of co-operation)
- pyrite (heals feelings of hurt suffered in past friendships)
- golden topaz (attracts friendships)

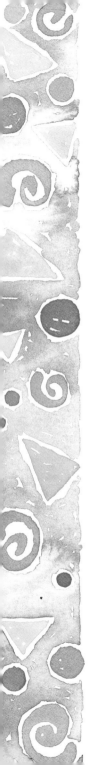

USING INTERIOR DECORATION TO ATTRACT
NEW CAREER OPPORTUNITIES

Cluttered hallways and rooms stop beneficial energy from circulating in your work life as well as in your home. If you want to create new work opportunities, or even if you just want to figure out what sort of work to do, you must clear clutter from the area of your home, workplace, bedroom or desk corresponding with your career aspiration. Use the feng shui house plan described on page 20 for your space, aligning it with the wall that contains the main doorway into the house or area.

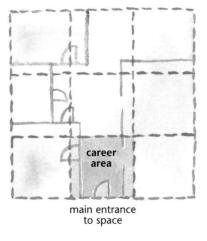

career
area

main entrance
to space

If you have a home office, clear this area of clutter to stimulate your career aspiration. Once you have tidied your home office and the area that corresponds to your career aspiration, use sound to encourage the energy to move through the area again, such as a wind chime hung in the area, or a hand bell rung there. Hand bells should not be hung up, because they need strong movement if they are to dispel negative or stagnant energy, and they can actually trap beneficial energy if they are left to stand in a room. Trapped beneficial energy very quickly converts into stagnant energy.

You can stimulate your career or redirect it beneficially if you decorate the career area of your home, workplace, office, bedroom, study or desk with appropriate symbols that resonate with the water element and its compatible element, metal. Decorative objects to use include small table or wall fountains, brass pots, and photographs or diplomas within metal frames. It is best to avoid symbols that relate to the element of earth, such as potted plants.

If you wish to enhance this aspiration further, keep a light burning in the chosen area. Change the light bulb promptly when it burns out, and make sure it is attractively covered, preferably with yang colors — reds, oranges and yellows. Leave a light on over your desk; this will symbolize clear insight into work-related issues. This practice will be especially useful if you are not sure in which direction your career should go.

TIPS TO ENCOURAGE GOOD LUCK IN JOB INTERVIEWS

When you are applying for a job, tie a black tassel to the handle of the briefcase you will be taking with you to the interview. (You could attach the tassel to the inside of the briefcase instead.) Make sure that your briefcase is black, with a gold-colored trim. In feng shui, black symbolizes endurance and strength, while gold symbolizes wealth and prosperity. To attract luck, consider also placing six I-Ching coins in the briefcase.
You could also use a nature magic charm. Make a small pouch out of a round piece of natural cloth, and place a black sapphire inside it. Carry the pouch with you to the interview to encourage new work.

Clearing Your Eating Space: the Kitchen and Dining Room

Clutter in the Kitchen: Lifestyle Choices

In feng shui, the kitchen is a symbol of your family's prosperity. It is also the place in the house where clutter most often accumulates. The cause may be the inhabitants' erratic lifestyles, reflected in irregular eating habits, or an unwillingness to cook. Clutter in this area represents the slowing down of the flow of abundance to you and your family.

If you never seem to have the time to use your kitchen, or often feel reluctant to use it, check to see whether the energy flow of the room is affected by poison arrows (see page 13). These may be directed either from the kitchen fittings or through the kitchen window. Straight-edged kitchen cabinets and open shelves are believed to create poison arrows that can cause a sense of ill health. If you have open shelving in the kitchen, consider adding doors to cover it.

Another feng shui issue to consider is your position while working in the kitchen. Does food preparation, cooking, or cleaning at the sink necessitate having your back to the door leading into the room? If you find that you can't get anyone to help you with the dishes, the reason may, at least in part, be the fact that being at the sink means having your back to the door. This makes you feel uncomfortable and apprehensive. As a remedy, place a mirror above the sink. Then you can see the door behind you. Use this feng shui cure above the stove, as well as in other important preparation areas that necessitate your facing away from the kitchen door.

Discomfort in the kitchen can also arise from the clash of two elements, fire and water. Water is detrimental to fire (see pages 18–19), so it is important to keep separate any appliances and fittings that symbolize these incompatible elements. If your sink is right next to the stove, you can use the element of wood to keep the flow of energy moving harmoniously. Consider placing a thick wooden chopping board or a set of decorative wooden shelves at right angles between the stove and the sink. To stabilize the chopping board, think of attaching a bracket onto the wall into which you can slide the board, to keep it on its side in an upright position.

Once you have eliminated the generation of negative energy, consider setting aside one full day for cleaning your kitchen from top to bottom and reorganizing the space. Before the big clean-up day, make a list of when and what you like to eat. Stock your pantry with ingredients that can be used to cook your favorite meals. Make a list of what you would like to bake, stir fry, or cook in some other way. Match this to the types of utensils you need.

Feng shui practitioners advise you to observe two important rules when you shop for utensils:

1 Buy the best quality utensils you can afford, as they will last longer, and this will also lessen the number of broken items in your home.

2 Make sure that your utensils match, as this will help create a sense of harmony while you cook.

Nature Magic Tip
~
COOKING WITH THE SEASONS
Consider clearing and restocking your pantry at the beginning of each season. The energies of each season correspond to different styles of cooking:

~ Spring
stir fries, quick cooking
~ Summer
broiling (grilling) and steaming
~ Autumn
stewing and baking
~ Winter
roasting, slow cooking

In nature magic, tapping into the energy of the seasons helps bring your health and energy back into balance.

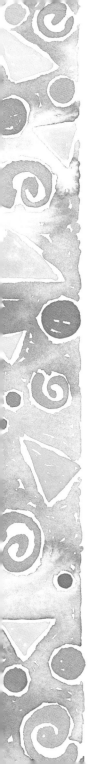

KEEPING YOUR STOVE AND SINK CLEAR:
ATTRACTING ABUNDANCE

The kitchen is one of the most important rooms for encouraging both abundance and inspiration into your home. There are two powerful elements at work in the kitchen — fire (symbolized by the stove) and water (symbolized by the sink and the refrigerator).

To create abundance within your life, keep both elements clean and ensure they are separate from one another. As leaking taps and pipes symbolize a waste of finances, make sure that these are kept in good condition and are repaired promptly. The stove should always be cleaned after use. Make sure that all burners work and that you use them all, in rotating order — preferably in a clockwise direction, for both the northern and southern hemispheres. Using all the burners, and not favoring one over another, will keep the energy circulating in the kitchen and in your finances.

In feng shui, it is important that the stove is well-positioned in the kitchen and in the house as a whole. Take note of the following principles:

- It should not face the door to the kitchen, or the front door
- It should ideally face in a south-easterly direction, or in the cook's favorable direction (see pages 78–79).

The sink must also be kept in pristine condition. The drain hole must be kept lightly covered by a sink plug at all times. As water is a symbol of wealth in feng shui, it is important that it does not drain away. Dirty dishes left in the sink are the worst kind of clutter, symbolizing not just an obstruction to generating prosperity in your life, but also 'dirt' in the family home, such as unhappy news or a lowering of status.

Keep detergent and other kitchen cleaning products out of sight, neatly organized in a convenient cupboard. Feng shui practitioners also advise having a pleasant view outside, or an inspiring picture to look at.

THE RITUAL OF DINING:
CREATING A HARMONIOUS SPACE

If family dinners have been less than harmonious, or dinner parties have not gone well, check whether the dining area is affected by a protruding interior wall, or whether a sharp angle from a pole or a neighboring house can be seen from the table.

If the table has been the scene of disharmony, perform the following ritual to cleanse the area of negative energy:

Step 1 Clear all debris from the table; wash all plates thoroughly and stack away neatly.

Step 2 Remove the tablecloth or place mats; hang outside for a couple of hours.

Step 3 Fill a metal bowl with tap water and add a small cup of hot water in which 2–3 tablespoons of salt (preferably sea salt) have already been dissolved.

Step 4 In a circular motion, clean the table down with the salty water. Don't worry about scratching the surface of your table — salt crystals that have not dissolved usually sink to the bottom of the bowl. As salt has a yang quality, it is very effective for restarting the flow of energy around the table.

Also consider the shape of your table. In feng shui, circular, oval or octagonal table tops will generate a beneficial and harmonious energy flow. Square tables are believed to create disharmony; this can be alleviated by the use of a 'lazy Susan' or a large circular bowl. To stimulate harmony at an important dinner party, especially if it is a business dinner, try to incorporate a circular table decoration that includes gold images, such as a golden pineapple.

In the West, when the pineapple was first introduced to dinner tables in the 18th century, it was regarded as the ultimate symbol of hospitality because of its costliness. In feng shui principles, the pineapple is a golden fruit that is symbolic of abundance and wealth.

For dinner gatherings, make sure that no one seated at the table has his or her back to the door leading into the room; anyone in this position may feel vulnerable or tense. Place a screen between the door and people seated at the dinner table whose backs are towards the door.

FENG SHUI TIP

To enhance abundance in your household, place a mirror in the dining room so that it reflects the food. This symbolizes the doubling of your prosperity. Many antique sideboards (especially those made in the 19th century) have mirrors in the backboards that gave the impression of extra food and utensils and used to double up as splashbacks for meat carving done at the sideboard. If you do have mirrors on your sideboard, make sure that you always keep them clean and free from dust and grime. Also check that the silver backing is not wearing off.

ENHANCING ROMANCE:
MUSIC, MAGIC AND CANDLELIGHT

If you are planning an intimate dinner for two, consider both feng shui and nature magic principles. To clear your table of previous negative associations, take a hand bell or another melodious bell and ring it over the table and the two chairs that you will be using for the dinner. Walk around the table in a continuous circular motion, and imagine all unhappiness from past relationships vanishing.

Then stop ringing, and take a deep breath. Does the area feel fresher? If it does, you can work on enhancing the atmosphere so that it is conducive to romance.

In feng shui, chairs are important considerations — make sure that they are comfortable, and positioned so that both of you can see the door. If you are covering the table with a cloth, make sure that it is freshly washed and that it does not need repairs.

Special feng shui decorations can be placed in the room where you are having dinner, such as a harmonious photograph showing both of you happy together. A photograph like this can also be used as part of the table decoration. You can scatter one or two of the following decorations around the room, or position them in the part of the room that corresponds with the relationship section of your feng shui house plan (see page 40):

- two ducks placed on a rounded mirror (to symbolize calm emotions)
- two pairs of chopsticks
- an image of a phoenix
- real or silk peonies.

Nature Magic Tip

~

Take a red candle and, with the sharp end of a clove, write your name and that of your dinner guest lightly down its side. As you are writing, visualize that the dinner you are preparing is going smoothly and that the energies between the two of you are flowing beneficially. When you have finished, push the clove into the candle at a point about an inch (2.5 cm) below the top of the candle. Light the candle as soon as your guest arrives. By the time you both sit down to dinner, the flame should have reached the clove and released its scent, as well as the spell you prepared earlier. Also remember, as you are preparing the meal, to visualize that the food is giving strength and happiness to your guest.

Dim the lights for your romantic dinner, as this creates a yin atmosphere suitable for romance. To balance the yin atmosphere, use yang-colored candles, such as red or pink, to enhance the energy flow in this area. Sounds can also be used to stimulate the flow of energy. However, remember that these should be melodious, and not too loud. Make a tape of your favorite music, and ensure that the names of the pieces are not negative (use your judgment — avoid titles such as 'Love's Despair'!).

Certain foods have been considered conducive to love for centuries — oysters, caviar, chocolate. In nature magic, potions and special love amulets can also be made. They should incorporate the following herbs and spices:

Cardamom ~ Cinnamon ~ Clove ~ Ginger ~ Lavender ~ Rose

Clearing Your Bathroom

Feng Shui Tips for Your Bathroom

In feng shui, the bathroom has a yin or female energy. Because of its relationship to the element of water, the state of your bathroom is also symbolic of your wealth. Interestingly, in nature magic water is symbolic of emotions, so the state of your bathroom is also an indication of your feelings. This is one of the reasons you should consider making the bathroom into a small sanctuary where you can wash away the troubles of the day (see pages 60–61) or relax and regain your strength and vitality (see pages 62–63).

Before the bathroom can be used for your own emotional cleansing, it needs to be cleansed itself. Set aside one day for reviving the energy of this room. Take out all clutter from drawers and cabinets. Separate what you do and don't need, and consider how you will store the necessary bathroom items so that they are kept tidy and contained.

Open the windows and door, wash all tiles with your favorite ecologically sound cleaner, and replace all towels and bath mats with new or freshly washed ones. If you can purchase new towels, consider buying yang-colored towels and shower and window curtains. Reds, oranges and other warm colors will help balance the yin function of the room.

Once the room is freshly cleaned, check the position of the toilet. In feng shui, the ideal position for the toilet is not in the bathroom at all, but in a separate room by itself. If your toilet is in the bathroom, place a wind chime in front of it to distract the attention of the energy flowing through the room.

The toilet is one of the strongest drains on beneficial energy in the home or business. Stand at the door of the bathroom. If the toilet is the first thing you see when you enter, place a flowering potted plant, such as an African violet, on the cistern, or position a statue on the floor next to the toilet. It is important always to flush with the lid down so that money — associated with the water element — is not symbolically flushed away. If your toilet is positioned in the wealth sector of your house, you will need to take extra precautions to make sure you do not lose money as soon as you make it. Use your feng shui house plan (see page 20), aligning it with the wall that contains the main doorway into the area. Check where your toilet is situated on this plan.

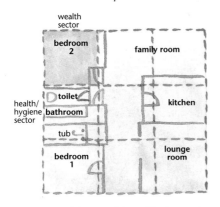

Auspicious position of bathroom/
toilet in the hygiene/health sector

Inauspicious position of bathroom/
toilet in the wealth sector

If the toilet is within your wealth sector, place a mirror on the toilet lid, on the wall behind the toilet or on the door to the bathroom. By positioning the mirror in one or all of these places, you are creating an illusion that the toilet is not really there. Try this for one week, and see if you experience a beneficial change in your finances.

FENG SHUI TIP

It is desirable for the bathroom to be positioned in the hygiene/health sector of your home or business.

This book predominantly focuses on the flow of energy through our environment, but it is important to realize that this energy also flows through our bodies, and is sensitive to our emotions. There is not much point in clearing, cleansing and uncluttering your external environment without looking within as well.

The holistic medical practices of such cultures as the Chinese and Indian have recognized for thousands of years that emotions and the energy they create within the body are important factors affecting our health. It is imperative not to hold on to negative or constrictive emotions, such as anger and frustration, but to release the stagnant energy these emotions cause.

In modern daily life, negative emotions will inevitably appear. However, you should consider implementing a daily or (if this is not possible) a weekly regime to help relieve your body of these emotions, so that the energy flows harmoniously through the body.

In nature magic, bathing can be used as a symbolic act to wash away the troubles and frustrations of the day. Visualization can be added to enhance the feeling of release. Try the following bathing ritual.

Make the atmosphere of the bathroom as pleasant and relaxing as possible. Light some candles — plain natural beeswax is ideal — and scent the room, preferably by burning some essential oils such as cedarwood (to stabilize the emotions), geranium (to cleanse the emotions) and lavender (to calm the emotions). Arrange a large, clean, fluffy towel and a generous glass of water near you while you are bathing. Choose your favorite scented soap or bubblebath.

Fill the bathtub or adjust the shower so that the water is a soothing temperature. As you step into the bathtub or shower, imagine that you are entering a fantasy world full of warm mists, waterfalls and intriguingly shaped islands. Feel the warm water on your skin, and relax into this new world. Let any anger just float past you — the emotion is not important any more in this warm, relaxing place.

Allow any thoughts of the day to drift past you, and watch them pop out of existence as the bubbles from your soap or bubble bath burst and disappear. Lie or stand in this relaxed state for as long as you like, remembering to take a sip from your glass of water now and then.

When you are ready, stand up in the tub or clean off the soap in the shower, and make a series of sharp sweeps with your hand over your hair, face, neck, shoulders, arms, torso, legs and feet. The idea is that you are sweeping any remaining negative energy away from your body. At the end of each sweep, flick your hand as if you are shaking the last vestiges of the energy from it.

If you have taken a bath, watch the water run down the drain as you are toweling yourself dry. Imagine that you are watching all your troubles wash down the drain, leaving you clean, fresh and happy.

RELAXING INTO AN UPLIFTING
PERSONAL CLEANSING

The personal cleansing described here focuses on activating the seven chakras (energy centers) of the body — at the base of the spine, a few fingers' width below the navel, a few fingers' width above the navel, the heart, throat, the middle of the forehead, and the crown of the head.

Bring to the bathroom a plain beeswax candle and a large glass of cool water. Fill a bathtub with soothingly warm water, or adjust the shower accordingly. Light the candle, and place it where you can see the flame comfortably without straining. If you are using the bathtub, use 2 to 3 drops of your favorite essential oil in the water, and relax each part of your body.

Feel the bottom of your spine connecting with the bottom of the bathtub, and imagine that the energy of your spine is spiraling down into the earth. Alternatively, if you are showering, feel your feet connecting with the tiles, and imagine that the energy of your spine is moving down through your feet and linking into the earth. This is an exercise called 'grounding'.

When you feel grounded, stare briefly at the lighted candle. Close your eyes and imagine that the light of the candle flame is at the base of your spine and that it is glowing red. Once you have anchored this image in your mind, open your eyes again to look at the candle. Then close them, and imagine that the light of the candle flame is now at a spot a few fingers' width below the navel, glowing orange. Now you have two areas of color shimmering at the same time.

Open your eyes to look at the candle flame, and repeat this procedure for the other five chakra points:

- a few fingers' width above your navel, imagine a yellow light
- at your heart, imagine a green light
- at your throat, imagine a blue light
- in the middle of your forehead, imagine a purple light
- on the crown of your head, imagine an indigo light.

Let these seven colors glow in your body. As these chakra points are important energy centers, by visualizing them glowing you are activating them to stimulate the flow of energy through your body. Some of these areas may feel congested or difficult to visualize. This indicates that you may have a blockage in the area. Either rub the area to stimulate circulation, or consider getting a soothing massage to disperse the blockage.

When you have activated all the energy centers and have felt them pulsing through your body without obstruction, imagine that you are dimming each light and allowing any blockage to flow down the spine and out into the earth to be safely dispersed. Once this is done, blow out the candle, and take a deep drink of water. Have a relaxing wash, and leave the bathroom feeling invigorated and vibrant.

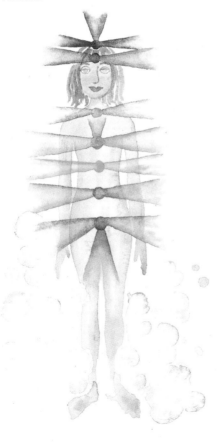

Nature Magic Tip

~

A nature magic method for imbuing your bathroom with a calming atmosphere is brushing your windows and doors with a few sprigs of lavender. Prepare for this by tying up aromatic lavender sprigs in a bunch, and placing this in a sunny place for an hour. Once the energy of the cut lavender has been revitalized by the sun, whisk the brush along the door and window frames of the bathroom with a flicking motion, imagining that the energy passing into the room is being enhanced by calm vibrations. This is a particularly effective way of cleansing if the view out of the bathroom door or window is unpleasant, or if a poison arrow is directed toward these openings.

Clearing Your Business Space at Home and at Work

Office-Warming: A Feng Shui Way of Ensuring Success in Business

Many Chinese businesses begin their life with an office-warming ceremony, to ensure their success and prosperity. Such ceremonies have been developed in feng shui to clear the space of any negative energy attached to it, and then attract beneficial qi to the workspace. The ceremony combines a cleansing of the business space with the lighting of a small, contained fire to symbolize the entry of the cosmic breath of the dragon — in other words, beneficial energy — into the office or business space.

In the Chinese culture, the time of birth is very important for working out whether a baby will be lucky or unlucky in life. Lucky and unlucky days and times can be determined by consulting the Tong Shu, or Chinese almanac. Similarly, the hour when a business begins its operation can have an effect on the general flow of clients to the business, which symbolizes the flow of beneficial energy to it.

The first step toward the ceremony is working out the lucky day and time for the commencement of your business at the new premises. Consult either the Tong Shu or a feng shui practitioner to ascertain the precise hour your business should start. There are many lucky days and times during the year, so all you need to do is choose the one closest to the day you are thinking of commencing your business.

Once the date and time have been set, work at getting everything ready for the start of business; clean and outfit the new premises, and get stock in. Once you have finished setting up your space (preferably the day before the ceremony), tape black paper, cardboard or cloth on all openings to the workspace, such as the doors, windows and air vents. Switch off all electrical appliances at least one

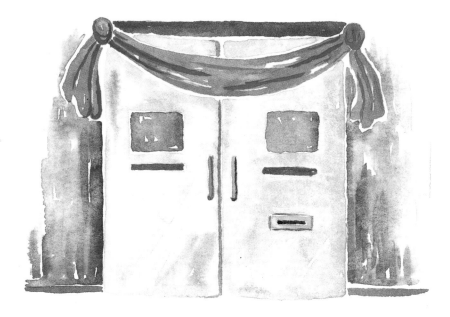

hour before the ceremony. When ready, gather all your staff outside the main entrance to the workspace.

Place a red sash or banner across the main entrance (preferably in the upper section or above the door), and light a small fire in a cauldron half filled with sand, or on a low, moveable charcoal stove. Stoke the fire. Assign one of your employees to be the timekeeper, and ask them to alert you when the auspicious time for the start of your business approaches. At the correct moment, place the cauldron or stove at the front entrance, right under the lintel, and carefully step over it, leading with your left foot. Each employee should then enter the premises by stepping over the fire, also leading with the left foot.

At this point, take the red banner down from the doorway, pull down the black coverings and start up the electrical appliances. Celebrate with music and a party. This will harmonize well with the nature magic tradition of sharing food to symbolize the bonding of a group of people.

Remember that you can consult a feng shui practitioner, or ask one to be on-hand to help guide you through this simple ritual.

CLEANSING THE HOME OFFICE

If you work from home, either occasionally or on a full-time basis, consider implementing a routine cleansing of your home office, preferably after a major project has ended or before planning to attract new clients. Some freelance workers find that they do this automatically, as they have an instinctive urge to 'clear the decks' before new work comes in. In both feng shui and nature magic, it is believed that the sheer act of clearing 'old energy' encourages 'new energy', sometimes in the form of new clients or work, to enter your life.

A cleansing in the home office can entail anything from tidying away your files or tools to rearranging the furniture. Make sure that your office space is dust free. Wipe down your tabletop. Tidy up your books, files, tools and equipment, and assess whether you need to store your past files in the office, or find off-site storage. Overwhelming clutter in the office can lead to an inability to carry your work through to a satisfactory conclusion. Keep your workspace as clear as possible of files or books representing past jobs. If you do not, you may find that your energy is caught up with the past.

There are a few feng shui principles that can help you regain a sense of balance in your work.

66

FENG SHUI PRINCIPLES FOR BALANCE IN YOUR WORK

1 Never have your desk or office space in your bedroom, because this will interfere with your sleep. If your desk is in your bedroom, separate the two areas with a screen, bookshelf or large plant.

2 Never sit at your desk or workbench with your back facing the door, because you may feel vulnerable and insecure in this position.

3 Move your desk to face your favorable direction (see pages 78–79), because you will then be able to tap into a beneficial energy flow.

4 Do not have shelves in the office unless they are covered by a cabinet door, because the shelves will generate 'poison arrows'.

5 If you have a choice, position your home office in your wealth, acknowledgment, career, mentor or knowledge areas (see page 20).

6 Do not face a blank wall. Position an inspiring picture (not a mountainscape) or words above your desk.

7 Make sure that the view from your home office is tranquil, because an overactive, or yang, view will be overstimulating, causing headaches and an inability to focus.

Music and Aroma to Help You Concentrate

Some scents and sounds stimulate the beneficial flow of energy, and have been used in many traditions to generate a suitable atmosphere for special activities and ceremonies. These sounds and smells, if used consistently for a special purpose, build up an association so that a certain aroma or sound comes to evoke a particular state of mind. For example, with nature magic, lighting candles and preparing a particular incense or essential oil can put you in a contemplative state of mind, allowing you to focus on your spiritual work.

A similar result can be achieved by creating a small ritual for yourself that will get you in the right frame of mind for concentrating fully on your work. This will help prevent the distractions of the world from interfering with your focus.

Experiment for yourself to see what works. At the end of a good workday, try to think back to what put you in the right frame of mind. Once you have worked out your 'system', consider whether sound, aroma or even the presence of a particular stone can help enhance the mood.

Clearing Your Head: Music For Improving Your Concentration

If you are working to a close deadline, listening to Gregorian chants can help to lower your stress levels. The slow, tranquil rhythms will remind you to breathe more deeply into your diaphragm. This will help relieve stress, because anxiety and panic are often closely related to shallow breathing or hyperventilation. To keep a clear head while working, consider listening to some Mozart (particularly his Sonata for Two Pianos in D Major, (K. 448)), Bach, Vivaldi or Haydn.

In feng shui, sound is considered particularly useful for stimulating beneficial energy. It is important that the sounds are melodious; think, for example, of the pleasant random tinkle of a wind chime. However, you could also consider playing a melodious piece of music while you work. Western scientists have been experimenting for a number of years in an attempt to understand the effect of music and harmony on our minds. It has been found that constant exposure to certain types of musical stimulation can raise our level of intelligence.

As with all things, balance is the key — too much music can lead to overstimulation. In feng shui terms, the music becomes too yang or 'aggressive' if it is played too loudly, or if the sound is too jarring. This type of music will cloud rather than stimulate your thought processes.

If playing music during your work time feels inappropriate, consider less intrusive methods of improving your focus. Check the table below for essential oils and stones that will help you concentrate. Stones placed on your work table or stroked periodically can noticeably assist concentration.

Essential oils for concentration	Stones to aid your memory
Basil	Agate
Bergamot	Amethyst
Cinnamon	Aquamarine
Frankincense	Cat's Eye
Lavender	Emerald
Rosemary	Onyx

Using Symbols to Attract Financial Success

In feng shui, a number of symbols can be used in either your home or your business to stimulate success in your life. An extensive range of symbols or 'lucky objects' has developed in China over the centuries. These symbols include objects such as coins, statues, vases and fans that are believed to attract beneficial energy or disperse negative energy. You can use the symbols in one of two ways.

The first technique requires you to clear the energy of the space at the point where you wish the symbol to be placed, or where you feel instinctively it should be placed. Clear away all the clutter, and clean or dust the area to allow the symbol to work with an unimpeded flow of energy. If you want to be more specific, you could place a chosen symbol in a particular aspiration area of your home, business, bedroom or desk. Use your feng shui house plan (see page 20) to ascertain where your wealth aspiration is situated in relation to your front door.

With the second method, you can hang or place the symbol above an area where clutter is congregating in your wealth sector, and let it help clear the energy around the clutter. If you use the symbol in this way, you will be amazed how you will soon become 'inspired' to clear the clutter away.

Symbols used to attract finance to an individual or a business should always be placed at or above eye level. The color of wealth symbols should be either gold or bright yellow. These colors are 'yang', or aggressive in energy, and should be used sparingly, as a highlight in your interior decoration. The colors can occur either naturally, as in a goldfish or a piece of yellow fruit, or as a gilded or bronze metal coin.

Although the element of metal is destructive to wood, the element that
resonates to the wealth aspiration, metal coins can be used sparingly to enhance
financial success, particularly if a red tassel is hung from the coin or series of
coins or if the coins are wrapped in red paper. It is believed that the color red
enhances the strength of the wealth symbol. Multiple-coin charms are always
tied together with red thread.

In feng shui, prosperity charms abound. They usually combine a number of
images that are thought to attract wealth and abundance. The images include
special Chinese words and charms, three-dimensional miniature versions of
animals thought to be lucky, such as fish, bats, and stags, and coins, bells and
tassels. The charms can be made from a wide variety of materials, ranging from
plastic to gold and jade.

CLEARING YOUR GARDEN THE FENG SHUI WAY

THE FLOW OF ENERGY IN YOUR GARDEN: FENG SHUI AND THE GARDENER

The principles of feng shui arose from the observation of nature by Chinese philosophers over a great number of years. Houses that followed these principles were found to act as beacons, attracting a beneficial form of energy. If you want energy to reach your own house beneficially, use the special features observed in the gardens designed following feng shui principles.

It is very important for the garden to be designed in curves, with winding paths, circular arches and curved garden beds. Straight lines create fast-flowing energy that is inauspicious. However, such lines can be softened by groundcover plantings, for example, rosemary or thyme, or by climbers, such as star jasmine, clematis and wisteria. In feng shui, aromatic plants are also believed to attract beneficial energy.

The garden must also contain a balance of yin and yang elements. The yin elements in the garden (those representing female energy) include dark, spiky-leaved trees and low shrubs, blue and white flowers, and space between the garden beds, such as the lawn. Yang elements (those representing male energy) include light, rounded-leaved trees and upright shrubs, red and pink flowers, and the bunching of plants within garden beds. According to some schools of thought, the front garden is considered to contain predominantly yang energy while the backyard corresponds to yin energy.

Your front yard, no matter how small, must always be kept in good condition.

Any clutter, dying trees or broken garden furniture will obstruct beneficial energy as it moves toward your front door and into your home.

Start on a program of revamping your garden, preferably according to the seasons (see pages 74–75). If you wish to do something immediately to improve the flow of energy to the front door, consider the following strategies:

- leaving the front porch light permanently on (use a lower wattage bulb to conserve energy)
- buying a new welcome mat
- placing two potted plants or flowers on either side of the front door
- painting the front door.

If you have no water features in your garden, consider incorporating one. Water fountains or ponds are considered important ways of circulating beneficial energy around your home. They can also be used as successful cures if there is a pole or busy street aimed straight at your front door. Do remember, however, that the fountain should be circular and the pond should be made to look as natural as possible.

The backyard should also be kept in good condition. Its function is to provide a sense of support. In feng shui, this support is related to the image of a mountain. A house should ideally be sited in such a way as to have its back facing a mountain. If your backyard is facing a valley, consider planting some trees or placing some heavy earthenware pots at the back of the yard.

FENG SHUI TIP

Here are some feng shui garden 'don'ts':

- do not have straight lines in the garden
- do not plant trees that require their tops to be trimmed (this symbolizes the cutting down of your potential)
- do not incorporate square or rectangular ponds.

If you have straight lines in the garden, consider adding circular pots, urns, stepping stones and statues to soften the edges of garden paths, walls and ponds.

HONORING THE SEASONS

In nature magic, the rise and fall of the energy of the seasons provides a structure within which magic can work. If we tap into the earth's energy and integrate its wisdom into our lives, we will find that we experience more happiness. We will be gaining a release from the enormous stress of trying to live our lives disconnected from the rhythms of nature.

Gardening can help achieve this release. Watching how the energy rises in spring, matures in summer, produces a harvest in autumn and then goes underground during winter will help you implement similar strategies in your life.

Many people who practice nature magic follow the Celtic myth of the 'Wheel of the Year', in which the cycle of the four seasons of spring, summer, autumn and winter is seen as a love story between a god and a goddess. Each season represents the birth, youth, old age and death of the Sun god. As the Sun god grows in strength during spring and summer, the Moon goddess becomes more retiring, but she gains energy when the Sun god reaches old age and death.

This myth echoes the strength of the Sun during the daytime and the visibility of the Moon during the night, and is also reflected in Chinese traditions concerning the seasons. In Chinese culture, the cycle is generated by the dynamic between yin (female) and yang (male) energies. There are five seasons in this culture: the four usual ones and 'late summer'. In the northern hemisphere, late summer occurs between 31 July and the autumn equinox in late September,

BEST TIME TO PLANT

The best time to plant is believed to be the period from the day after the new moon to the day before the full moon. Some believe that planting on the actual day of the new moon or the full moon is inauspicious. However, herbs for spells involving new love or for assuring the success of new ventures can be cut on the night of the new moon. Herbs for spells about protection or healing should be cut on the night of the full moon.

and in the southern hemisphere it occurs between 31 January and the autumn equinox in late March. This period represents a harmoniously equal balance between yin and yang energies.

Recommended garden activities through the seasons

Nature magic festivals	Northern hemisphere dates	Southern hemisphere dates	Related garden activities
Winter solstice (Yule)	21–23 December (date varies)	21–23 June (date varies)	Clear fallen branches; plan out paths and garden beds.
Height of winter energy (Candlemas/Imbolc)	2 February	1 August	If you have no snow, lay out paths, set out garden beds and put mulch on them; repair fences, pergolas or garden furniture.
Spring equinox (Ostara)	21–23 March (date varies)	21–23 September (date varies)	Build a small space to nurture seedlings; plant yang-colored flowers and herbs.
Height of spring energy (May Day/Beltane)	1 May	31 October	Clean out tool shed and tools; remove clutter in garage; make an efficient workspace for all garden tools.
Summer solstice (Litha)	21–23 June (date varies)	21–23 December (date varies)	Create a space for friends to gather; clean, repair or install garden furniture.
Height of summer energy (Lammas)	1 August	2 February	Create a spiral garden with a pond in the center.
Autumn equinox (Mabon)	21–23 September (date varies)	21–23 March (date varies)	Prepare plantings for spring; clear a space for quiet meditation on the bounty of the garden.
Height of autumn energy (Halloween/Samhain)	31 October	1 May	Rake, clear and mulch; prune where necessary, and clear clutter in the garden shed in preparation for winter.

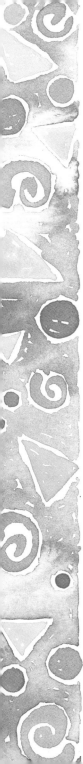

GLOSSARY

Bagua – a grid system with eight squares representing eight aspects of life identified in the I-Ching and applied in the art of feng shui, as well as a ninth square, in the center, which represents the energy of earth.

Beltane – a major Celtic festival marking the height of spring's energies (also known as May Day).

Candlemas – a major Celtic festival marking the height of winter's energies (also known as Imbolc).

Carnelian – a red-orange stone renowned for its metaphysical ability to cleanse negativity.

Chakras – a series of energy centers running through the middle of the body.

Chi – see qi.

Feng shui – the Chinese art of placement and design to enhance the flow of universal energy.

Feng shui house plan – the overlay of a nine-square grid (the bagua — see above) over the plan of a residential or commercial site.

Halloween – a major Celtic festival marking the height of autumn's energies (also known as Samhain).

I-Ching – a complex, poetic method of divination developed in China many centuries ago (also known as the *Book of Changes*).

Imbolc – see Candlemas.

Lammas – a major Celtic festival celebrating the height of summer's energies.

Litha – a Celtic festival celebrating the summer Solstice (also known as Midsummer's Eve).

Mabon – a Celtic festival celebrating the autumn Equinox.

Nature magic – a term used in this book to refer to magical practices derived from the observation of nature and its forces (earth, air, fire and water) — see page 9.

Ostara – a Celtic festival celebrating the spring Equinox.

Poison arrow – a harmful shaft of energy created by long straight corridors, paths or roads, or by sharp angles in or outside the home.

Qi – the Chinese name for universal energy (also known as chi).

Samhain – see Halloween.

Smudging – the Native American art of cleansing space by the burning of a smudge stick, often made from the herb sage.

Tong Shu – a Chinese almanac listing, among other things, lucky and unlucky days.

Yang – male or extroverted energy.

Yin – female or introverted energy.

Yule – a Celtic festival celebrating the winter Solstice.

GUIDE TO THE CHINESE CALENDAR AND FAVORABLE DIRECTIONS

To use the Chinese Calendar on the following pages, look up the year of your birth. For example, if you were born in 1963, before January 25, your year of birth in the Chinese Calendar would be 1962. If you were born in 1963 on or after January 25, the entries for 1963 will tell you your predominant element, and the most favorable direction for sitting at your desk or sleeping in your bed. The directions for each year differ according to whether you are male or female. For example, a female born on January 26, 1963, should sit at her desk facing south-west or sleep facing north-east. A male born in the same year should work facing south-east and sleep facing north.

The Chinese Calendar and Favorable Directions

New year date	Element	Female favorable directions for luck	Female favorable directions for sleep	Male favorable directions for luck	Male favorable directions for sleep
1930 Jan 30	Metal	SW	NE	NW	W
1931 Feb 17	Metal	E	S	W	NW
1932 Feb 6	Water	SE	N	NE	SW
1933 Jan 26	Water	NE	SW	N	SE
1934 Feb 14	Wood	S	E	S	E
1935 Feb 4	Wood	N	SE	NE	SW
1936 Jan 31	Fire	SW	NE	SE	N
1937 Feb 11	Fire	W	NW	E	S
1938 Jan 31	Earth	NW	W	SW	E
1939 Feb 19	Earth	SW	NE	NW	W
1940 Feb 8	Metal	E	S	W	NW
1941 Jan 27	Metal	SE	N	NE	SW
1942 Feb 18	Water	NE	SW	N	SE
1943 Feb 5	Water	S	E	S	E
1944 Jan 25	Wood	N	SE	NE	SW
1945 Feb 13	Wood	SW	NE	SE	N
1946 Feb 2	Fire	W	NW	E	S
1947 Jan 22	Fire	NW	W	SW	NE
1948 Feb 10	Earth	SW	NE	NW	W
1949 Jan 29	Earth	E	S	W	NW
1950 Feb 17	Metal	SE	N	NE	SW
1951 Feb 6	Metal	NE	SW	N	SE
1952 Jan 27	Water	S	E	S	E
1953 Feb 14	Water	N	SE	NE	SW
1954 Feb 3	Wood	SW	NE	SE	N
1955 Jan 24	Wood	W	NW	E	S
1956 Feb 12	Fire	NW	W	SW	NE
1957 Jan 31	Fire	SW	NE	NW	W
1958 Feb 18	Earth	E	S	W	NW
1959 Feb 8	Earth	SE	N	NW	SW
1960 Jan 28	Metal	NE	SW	N	SE
1961 Feb 15	Metal	S	E	S	E
1962 Feb 5	Water	N	SE	NE	SW
1963 Jan 25	Water	SW	NE	SE	N
1964 Feb 13	Wood	W	NW	E	S
1965 Feb 2	Wood	NW	W	SW	NE
1966 Jan 21	Fire	SW	NE	NW	W
1967 Feb 9	Fire	E	S	W	NW
1968 Jan 30	Earth	SE	N	NE	SW

New year date	Element	Female favorable directions for luck	Female favorable directions for sleep	Male favorable directions for luck	Male favorable directions for sleep
1969 Feb 17	Earth	NE	SW	N	SE
1970 Feb 6	Metal	S	E	S	E
1971 Jan 27	Metal	N	SE	NE	SW
1972 Feb 15	Water	SW	NE	SE	N
1973 Feb 3	Water	W	NW	E	S
1974 Jan 23	Wood	NW	W	SW	NE
1975 Feb 11	Wood	SW	NE	NW	W
1976 Jan 31	Fire	E	S	W	NW
1977 Feb 18	Fire	SE	N	NE	SW
1978 Feb 7	Earth	NE	SW	N	SE
1979 Jan 28	Earth	S	E	S	E
1980 Feb 16	Metal	N	SE	NE	SW
1981 Feb 5	Metal	SW	NE	SE	N
1982 Jan 25	Water	W	NW	E	S
1983 Feb 13	Water	NW	W	SW	NE
1984 Feb 2	Wood	SW	NE	NW	W
1985 Feb 20	Wood	E	S	W	NW
1986 Feb 9	Fire	SE	N	NE	SW
1987 Jan 29	Fire	NE	SW	N	SE
1988 Feb 17	Earth	S	E	S	E
1989 Feb 6	Earth	N	SE	NE	SW
1990 Jan 27	Metal	SW	NE	SE	N
1991 Feb 15	Metal	W	NW	E	S
1992 Feb 4	Water	NW	W	SW	NE
1993 Jan 23	Water	SW	NE	NW	W
1994 Feb 10	Wood	E	S	W	NW
1995 Jan 31	Wood	SE	N	NE	SW
1996 Feb 19	Fire	NE	SW	N	SE
1997 Feb 7	Fire	S	E	S	E
1998 Jan 28	Earth	N	SE	NE	SW
1999 Feb 16	Earth	SW	NE	SE	N
2000 Feb 5	Metal	W	NW	E	S
2001 Jan 24	Metal	NW	W	SW	NE
2002 Feb 12	Water	SW	NE	NW	W
2003 Feb 1	Water	E	S	W	NW
2004 Jan 22	Wood	SE	N	NE	SW
2005 Feb 9	Wood	NE	SW	N	SE
2006 Jan 29	Fire	S	E	S	E

Published by Lansdowne Publishing Pty Ltd
Sydney NSW, Australia
© Copyright 2000 Lansdowne Publishing Pty Ltd
Commissioned by: Deborah Nixon
Production Manager: Sally Stokes
Text: Antonia Beattie
Text pp. 14-15, 34-37: Patti Dacey
Feng Shui Consultant: Rosemary Stevens
Cover illustration: Tina Wilson
Illustrator: Jane Cameron
Designer: Sue Rawkins
Editor: Avril Janks
Project Co-ordinator: Kylie Lowson

National Library of Australia Cataloguing-in-Publication-Data
       Beattie, Antonia.
       The feng shui guide to clearing your space: how to
       unclutter and balance your environment using ancient cleansing
       rituals.
       ISBN 1 86302 719 X.
       1. Feng-shui. I. Title.
       133.3337

Set in Stempel Schneidler on QuarkXPress
Printed in Singapore by Tien Wah Press (Pte) Ltd